America Stabbed James T Kirk In The Arm With A #2 Pencil

America Stabbed James T Kirk In The Arm With A #2 Pencil

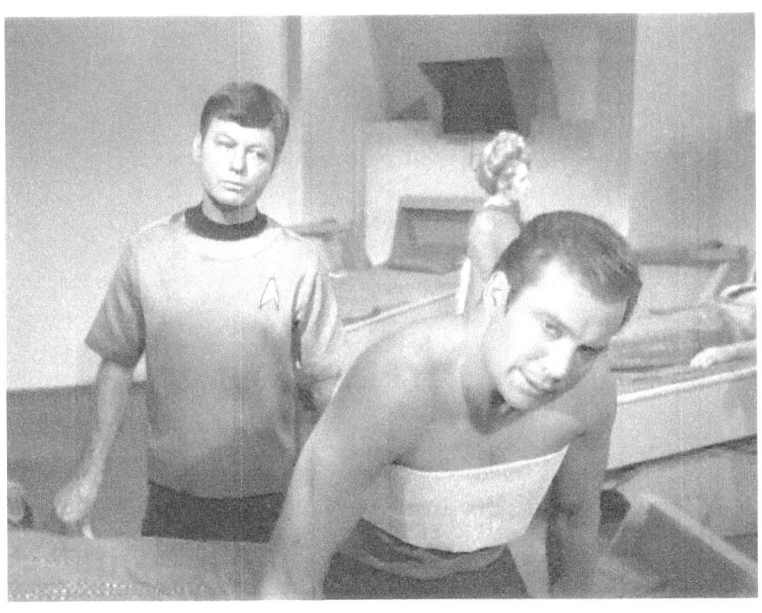

Poems By Jeanette Powers

Kung Fu Treachery Press
Rancho Cucamonga, CA
kungfutreacherypress.com

Copyright 2018 by Jeanette Powers
ISBN: 978-1-946642-61-5
LLOC: 2018951750

font: verdana
designer: Jeanette Powers
editors: Crista Siglin, Lissa Roads, Paul Koniecki
cover photos & interior photos: Star Trek
season 2, episode 10: Journey to Babel

contact Jeanette @ stubbornmulepress@gmail.com
@novel_cliche @drawwithyoureyesclosed
jeanettepowers.com

table of contents

Stab James T Kirk in the Arm
Myths of the Meglomania of Noise
Trashpeople Just Wanna Have Fun
Jump Off the World Trade Center
God is an Absentee Father & Late on Child Support
America has Daddy Issues & That's Why We Fuck
Butt Chugging the Kool-aid
Some Mothers are Quicker with a Scolding
Break Your Arm on His Cock
Campaign Champagne Enema
Minimum Efficiency Standards at the Guillotine
The Birds Have the Right Idea
All Righty All Mighty Whitey Rape Away
Enterprising Children Get A+'s

— find your own answers, captain —

"Interesting."
--everyone

STAB JAMES T KIRK IN THE ARM
WITH YOUR #2 PENCIL

in America no one finds themselves
in college again and taking a final exam
no one finds out it's a Scantron
and that it is so so easy
everyone can't find a #2 pencil
everyone can't fill in the dots
I do though it is so so easy
I finish first and leave the room
the rest of the campus though
has already graduated
because they don't need to fill in
they don't need to do finals
they don't need to do these things that I do
things I need to do because I was told to
they just need to laugh at each other
and with each other effortlessly
they just need to edge a squealing mean
they just need to regurgitate the memes
they ate on their feed that day
I go to my teacher's office
and realize everyone has been cheated

MYTHS OF THE MEGLOMANIA OF NOISE

what's another transgender
school shooter
in the bathroom
of your Catholic school yard
what's another Rifleman
holding hostage
a theater full of superhero fans
what's another building
brought to the ground
by someone who's decided
he doesn't like where you stand
what's another child caught
in Poison Control crossfire

nothing but rats out there

what's your trauma about
what's your abuse about
why do you perpetuate this
why do you take pride in this
how many five star ratings
can you get on craigslist

for how you've been harmed today
sold a shotgun by listing it as a stereo
sold in an hour ahhhhh

can you cry some more
can you cry out onto
happy that your voice is heard
doesn't it make you amazed
delighted that people care

almost like you do the things together
you go buy the things together
what's another African Child
dying of thirst next to the Nile
what's another Indonesian Child
with a round belly looks so full
what's another American TV STAR
American 1000k likes running over there
to do some half-wit marathon right now

what's another Penny out of your pocket
what's another scroll to skim past everything

what's another school shooter
they aren't taking aim on you

"I don't know how much longer I'm going to be able to stand this.
I feel like my neck is in a sling."
--Bones

TRASHPEOPLE JUST WANNA HAVE FUN

one two three four five six
seven eight nine 10 11 12 13 14 15 16
700 17 thousandmillion carstruckssemiautomatics
divebombing deliveries over this bridge
this bridge is the loudspeaker to the city
louder than the river flowing underneath
than the water from which it springs
the water that they drink is
the water that you pollute
that you put your disinfectant into
your bitchass condom trashcan lifestyle into

you are a styrofoam culture
you are nothing more than something
to put in the trash can
if everything you own
is put into the trash
if the trash can you own
is put into the trash can
into the dumpster then
I want you to imagine your
love affair with a garbage pile

I want you to lay down in the dumps
I want you to finger the coffee grinds
and rub them on your nipples
I want you to take that dirty diaper
and wear it like a face mask

I want you to accept what you produce
you are the makers of detritous assholery
the makers of another lost continent of goods
you are the Reapers of Earth
so that you can have another plastic bag
with tin foil wrapped plastic food

you are another clothing item
made by the hands of tiny hands of girls
somewhere across the globe

you don't see this
all of your commercials
are filmed in the suburbs
all of your commercials feature
smiling faces with perfect white teeth

the product of so many

thrown away plastic toothbrushes
so many whitening products
sold to you
sold to you
sold to you
sold to you
sold to you
sold to you
sold to you
sold to you
sold to you
sold to you
sold to you

to be so white
to be white to be clean
means to make heaping
infinities of trash
means to the loot the world
to pollute the earth

that is to say to destroy
yourself aloofly
because you cannot separate
yourself from that of which you were born

logically and effectively."
--Spock

JUMP OFF THE WORLD TRADE CENTER

the city is noir black and white everything
makes sense everything is opposite
gravity is levity
right is might
money is happiness
I'm above a skyscraper whose roof is an ocean
in the building are a window and a staircase
the clouds are the sky are ominous and inviting
the mood is all cough black no turning back
it is day in the far-away brightness of the sky
the proverbial 10000 pigeons with long strings
are flocking there like loose balloons
the pigeons are just like forever flying
just in reach of where I pinwheel
I turn to I don't know who
I don't know who to turn to
if you stand up you could start to bleed again
and I said it feels like my neck is in a sling
and I asked how can I pass this up
I'll eat I grab a bundle of strings
I'm 3-2-1 liftoff where-no-man-has-gone-before
this newest unknown final frontier

GOD IS AN ABSENTEE FATHER AND LATE ON CHILD SUPPORT

in America a woman is not allowed to be angry
not allowed to be angry about having a child
she's not allowed to have an abortion
without patriarchal interventionist strategies
she's not allowed to have an abortion
without judgement without persecution
without having to tell her story as though she's in
the normally she must be a groundbreaker
if she didn't want to be pregnant
a man however is allowed an escape hatch
abandon all children fear ye who enter here
for the father's will be God Damn
dead and gone we learn this
from your fucked god
his absentee *yes, kill it*

I said it your God is an absentee father
and he's taught us all that we
can all be *nowhere man don't listen*
he taught us that we should have a stepfather
he taught us that the virgin mother

should dedicate her life
and be nothing more than a mother to a son
a son who will be allowed
to abandon all who trust him
Abandon All who put their Faith in him
and yet Jesus was a *great guy man*
Jesus was my homeboy
Jesus was a Super Cool Dude
who told everyone to get rid of the money changers
and dressed in sandals and had long hair
and wander the land and didn't need anything
besides fealty and fuckery
and what that meant in the end
was that if he were to forgive you
it would mean he
would have been and you could be now pure

but what happened to Mary
we have no idea
and that's what America stands for
and that's what western Europe stands for
and that's what the troops stand for
and that's what each of my
American women must do
now they must stand for standing up for their

not children
they're not allowed to abandon
they must take the responsibility
they must take every one
of them under their skirts

American Women
Earth Women
are not allowed to be free
they are not allowed to chase their dreams
if it means a child gets in the way
but boy howdy little boy man
is it ever everything okay for you dude
to do what you want
no matter how many children
no matter how many women

everyone dies
you drone strike
you fucked twat
you killer of anything that matters

plug in another pacifier
work another two full time jobs
like a girl like a girl like a girl does

AMERICA HAS DADDY ISSUES AND THAT'S WHY WE FUCK

hey Daddy
hey Daddy where you been all my life
hey Daddy
Let Me Fall to your knees
hey daddy where you been all my life
you've been absent, mom is crying
mother's crying over
their mother doesn't have the energy
to take care of me my sister my brother
my three brothers the ten cousins
the 15 other children down the block
we're all gathering together like a bunch of fierce
Feral Hooligans because we're all children of neglect
we're all siblings of dissonance because Daddy
hey Daddy
daddy where you been where you're gone
and I'm not going to lie to you, I swear
be back in ten minutes hardy har har
man
and that's not good for any a buddy man
daddy you're making us into you
someone who'll never be there for us

"Devote yourself to reasons of passion or gain, those are reasons for murder."
--Andorian Fellow

BUTT CHUGGING THE KOOL-AID

America
you stepped on your own dick
and made yourself unable to get a hard-on
anymore

America
your fetishes have become
so kinked that your dick won't respond
to anything less than your phasers
on standby ready to fire at your order
into a black lives matter rally
your dick won't get hard
for anything less than
than a pepper spray cannon
at a *not my president* protest

America
your dick is soft for justice
hey John Wayne whip out your big ten inch
on that dirty lesbian heathen and make em
eat up those cowboy meat and potatoes
Captain Kirk won't eat!

he's a pussy vegetarian on another plane

America
your dick won't get hard
until there's blood on the ground
you want me to choke on your dick
so you stick a firecracker in the ass
of Dr Spock and of Oprah Winfrey
and Al Gore and Kevin Spacey
you want to stick a pudding pop in my ass
you want to stick a gat in the ass
of a trans woman
but only after she's left
beaten in the dirt

America
until you have fucked
everyone in the butthole
with your bayonet
so hard their intestines
start coming out of their bellybuttons
you aren't gonna be done
and no other gonna
live long or prosper
they're gonna gag

America
that's when you get
nice and good and hard

when you are eating the bleeding ass
of a minimum wage worker
you like children in cages at the border
fuck their families like a wife
you are about to rape
you stick it right in
and you stick it in good
you got a gun in your hand
a gun a gun
a gonna
you got a bad ass
machine gun penis
in your hand
you gonna go
pop
pop
pop
pop
pop

splat

"Mother, I cannot."
--Spock

SOME MOTHERS ARE QUICKER WITH A SCOLDING

my mother is her young self
she is blonde
high cheekbones and beautiful
but I am meet at this age
but I am me at the age I am

I have a round face
no eyebrows
she is beautiful and getting ready to go out
she has a reason to go out
because she is a craved and coveted thing
I have a reason to stay in because
I because I am the precipice of indifference
she is beautiful and getting ready to go out
but I am watching her boil three pots of water
she has nothing to do with this boiling water

I tell her
I have her figured out
but she would rather meat me
she says *you've got me all figured out*

and begins to put on another pot of water
she pours the other three boiling pots
over my head

her cheekbones cut the ice
my face melts like an off-brand crayon

I become rotund
with the surrendering waxy skin

I am four years old
and don't know yet
that you'll have to kill me
because the beating
just won't work
I carry
the burn scar
concentric rings
electric stove coil
red hot on my left palm

I say
I say
I have you figured out

BREAK YOUR ARM ON HIS COCK

pulling a gun and wide-eyed
he says "you're dead "
he puts the gun deep into my mouth
imagines the gun is his cock
and he puts it deep into my mouth
my mouth salivates around the gun
there is the taste of Steel
there's the taste of burnt life
I say "my name is Jeanette Powers
I have a son and a dog
please don't do this.
Krindy, Krindy is the girl
who laughed at me
when I broke my arm
trying to balance
on top of the fire hydrant."

everything goes black
no one called for help

help!

CAMPAIGN CHAMPAGNE ENEMA

you are the fattest person I have ever seen
at ... at 5 foot 7 and 115 pounds
you put on a whole 2nd person worth of product
you are not your roots you are Clairol Brown
you are not your eyes you are your sunglasses
you are not your lips you are collagen
covered in sassy red hall pass to beautiful piss
you are not your obedient or wild heart
you are the pair of fake tits size DD
your husband's hands do not touch your body
they touch balloons surgically inserted
beneath your skin got under your skin
anything to keep you you you away
to keep you distant
to keep everyone from figuring out
that you are not what you seem
that you are not capable of living up
to the seasonless constancy of the ad campaign
from figuring out that you have a bunion
a broken heart, stretch marks, pock marks
you can't live up to the commercial:
imagine a picture of white sand, white teeth
White America with white faces and white teeth

on white sand beaches and they're on vacation
and they are always smiling
they're all always happy and
the dishes are always done
and the children are playing tetherball
without being reminded of swinging fists
and the children are playing hide and seek
and they don't know what it feels like
to not want to be found
they are not broken arm hiding
and they are playing dress up laughing
together and not at just how fat magazine is
telling them they need to be thin as a razor blade
so that they look like the children on the television
they are television children and you
you are telling yourself you are fat when you are
so so thin but let me tell you this you consume you
you consume you
what you think they think you think
about what you think you think they think
you are name brand, not your feet but
a high heel that mutilates
you are stepping through your children's throats
they can't speak don't speak unless spoken to

by slogans and jingles you are not a personality
you are an ad campaign you are not a birdsong
you are a 30 second jingle, you are second place
taking a plate full of seconds to fill up
on how will we strive to be the best the best
how we strive to be the best a man can get
gillette is it best for you to keep getting fat so fat
fill up on these fulfillments of the cash man
ad man campaign champagne enema
then reach around and give it to your children
you put them in front of the television
you put them in front of the magazine
you say this is what you're supposed to look like
there will be no dishes in the sink
there will be oil change on your car every
2000 miles there will be the brushed hair
and the perfect ponytail and perfect cat eyeliner
you will be a cheerleader corporate lawyer
you will be the joy of cash register ca-ching
you are not fat on your white rice cakes
you are not fat on the Wonder Bread
you are fat on chip or swipe rotating balance
losing balance fall on your own card
you are not what you eat
you are what you buy

MINIMUM EFFICIENCY STANDARDS AT THE GUILLOTINE

think of your house
Roofing Plumbing electricity
think of your connections
internet worldwide telephone power
everything is going so fast
everything's got a deadline
everything's got a tracking number
you've got a tracking number
he's got a clock inside you
got a barcode sku isbending
your way to making your way
to pay the rent for that machine made
runaround paycheck to paycheck

think of your clothes
that traveled further across the world
then you have even been

THE BIRDS HAVE THE RIGHT IDEA

I was in my mother's house
it was an apartment it wasn't a house
it was a place we haven't been before
we were many places
we can never have been before

I was a teenager
she was full of rage
she was yelling at me
she was telling me something about
how I couldn't be believed
how I couldn't be taken seriously
she was telling me
I'd never be good enough
she was telling me without saying it
that she didn't love me

and I found these razor blades
and I took these razor blades to my skin
to the skin of the palm of my left hand palm
I held the razor blade in my right hand
and I repeatedly slash and slashed

and slash each time I lift
and opening up the palm
opening up the tendons
the ligaments the ways
that I can never reach out
and grab a thing again
and then I collapse
to the fingers around the blood
squeaking and squealing out of my hand

and I ship my fisted her
I ship my fisted her

and suddenly I was in the sky
careening like the starlings
I dream about
I was cleaning up and threw
I was beyond everything
everything that could have
been possibly blue
it was a definition of blue
I'd never seen before

I flew through windows effortlessly

I flew through buildings effortlessly
I couldn't go as high as I wanted
but I could go anywhere
but no matter how far and beautifully
and freely I flew careless carefree without
landing

I kept having to come back
to that dreary apartment complex
that demoralized apartment complex
my mother lived in
and I would pick up
through the ventilation chambers

I would pick up through the water pipes
and I would look into see that man
(it was me)
and his hand was healed
(my hand was healed)

there were no more injuries
but there was still a razor blade
and she would be yelling
about how she wasted her life on him

(me)
about how she'd wasted all of her beauty
and youth and how
she could've been a star
except for him
(me)
about how she'd
been strapped
and straddled and fucked
when she didn't wanna

and forced to raise this child

and spread her legs
she didn't anticipate
having to raise on her own
because that's not how they did it
in her grandfather's time
when shit gone done right
and he held his head

(I watched as I held my head)

and I watched him and I thought

that's not like him
(me)
it's not like him to be so upset
it's not like him to hurt himself
it's not like him to hurt myself
and be battered by this woman
it's not like him
to put a razor blade
in my right hand

and slash
and slash and slash
apart my left fist
it's not like me
to slash apart my left fist
with a razor blade
and clutch the bleeding arteries
spilling the red carpet
invitation down my wrists

while I shook my fist at the wind of her
while I shook my fist at the fight of her

or while she told me

I was worthless
but she told me
I wasn't wanted
why was why
she screamed at me
about as long as we
were under her roof
and then we would cry
and I would fly again
fly to places
where people flew
and the people who flew
would say
that they've never seen
someone

who was such a natural
at flying away like I do

how was such a natural
at catching the lift of the wind
and letting my wings spread
stuck in the vents
of an apartment complex

but I would think of him
and I would remember me
and I can't remember
how we got there
and it was probably
maybe it was someone's else
someone else's apartment
not my house
because
I think
that's so unlike me
to just be caught crying
there like that I

it's just
so unlike me to
just me

to just stand there
and openly bleed

ALL RIGHTY ALL MIGHTY WHITEY RAPE AWAY

god fuck faggot suck rapist cuck
God you are the worst thing I can think of

!not Jesus he's my homeboy!

wait man Jesus is Way Cool
the bible tells me so
God you are a sadistic sociopath psychopath
and I mean that as a diagnosis

God is the cruelest thing I can imagine
God killed more men than Satan
if you're happy and you know it clap your hands

God made woman be second
God made man and woman sibling
fucked each other from the Garden of Eden
it's his incestuous rapist pornographer God desire
just wanting everyone fucking and killing
and reflecting his being *you know*
that all of this murder on the Western Front

is because we learned it by watching you, *God*

you would invent moral cretins
you slithering fuck
and I say I hate everyone of you
that keeps saying that I should listen
to this immoral psychopath
because I don't want
to have Abraham kill Isaac
to prove he loves someone above the knife edge

I don't need a burning bush
I need a gynecologist
and now-a-days we've got pills for things like that
if you're obedient and ya know it clap your hands

God, you immoral cuckolding fuck
raping Mary like that
and everyone applauds
everyone applauds
why do you think people feel they have the right
to rape a woman now
because God, you told them it's okay

god god dammit

you are the greatest most
powerful curse word there is
because there is no limit to your rage
your condemnation
to your vindication
to your vitriol
to your revenge
there is no mercy to your
fight till your dead
no holds barred
if she's your wife you can rape her
no graven images because
no paper trail bitches
you have taught her
that when you are all-powerful
you can do whatever you want
without consequences
and that you cannot be questioned

and that is the worst thing
you could teach a world

ENTERPRISING CHILDREN GET A+'S

James T Kirk is not the captain
of the starship enterprise
Jamie Kirk is a boy in the third grade class
of a private school with low property taxes
but mostly rich children and a few charity cases
so that there is always someone to look down on
all the boys must wear pants
all the girls must wear skirts
girls who don't wear skirts
are to be mocked and scorned
boys who wear skirts aren't heard of in 1983
James T Kirk sits quietly
because he would like to wear a skirt
he sits next to you who have nothing at home
you who have an empty refrigerator
you who just needs to prove to this teacher
that you are worth loving
you who feels they have figured out
that the only way you will ever be loved
is by being smart enough
but there's this thing inside of you

you are a 3rd grader instructed
to memorize the Ten Commandments
you want to fight with Eric Fisher
because you like him and because
he might be smarter than you and you
want to be the smartest kid in the third grade class
you do not memorize the Ten Commandments
faster than Eric Fisher you are not the best cadet
you make 100% on all of your spelling tests
because you've been cheating
you do not want to tell people
you don't know how to spell the word MOUNTAIN
you do not want to tell people
you do not know how to spell the word RECEIVE
you do not want to tell people
that you've never been hugged
you do not want to tell people
that no one says I love you
you do not want to tell people
you are a latchkey kid and sometimes
mother doesn't come home
you want to get a hundred percent
on every spelling test
and memorize the Ten Commandments first
    Jamie Kirk sits next to you in that class

and he has Shaggy blond hair that's grown
a little too long because he cries whenever mother
says "let's get a haircut, son"
he cries because she is calling him son
you cry because no one calls you son
or daughter or anything else
Eric Fisher is the smartest boy in the class
and you are jealous of him
he has done everything better than you this year
and so one day you walk to the front of the class
and you commit to doing a radical thing
you walk to the front of class and turn
to face your classmates and you let your face fall
blank as a new spelling test page
and you begin to speak in tongues
because this is a Christian School
and you are a charity case
and you can't have the nice shoes
you have to wear pants and be ridiculed
you can't have the nice backpack
you don't have a tape deck
you have a radio at your grandpa's house
and you walk to the front of the class
and you've determined
you are going to do this thing

you are in the third grade and you tell
your first big lie standing at the front of the class
your mouth
you move your mouth
move your mouth in strange ways
you are faking speaking in tongues
you are a gibberish monster with dead eyes
you say to yourself:
    remember the no words
    try to not say any word
    your mouth is an instument you can't play
somehow to your horror you realize
the word "spaghetti" has slipped in
you're sure that Mrs. Griggs is going to notice
you're sure that you're going to be sent
to the office again, going to be mocked again
you're sure that you're going to be accused again
you are going to be sent to the principal's office
where they are going to insist
that God could never love a LITTLE GIRL LIKE YOU
not with those used shoes
not with that poor house
YOU KNOW EVERYONE GETS WHAT THEY DESERVE
and I stand in front of the class
    I mean you stand in front of the class

you are faking that God is speaking through you
you stop faking and return to your seat
and pretend to wake up from a lethargy
although you don't know that word yet
your breath is held, you don't know
what will happen and then
the class applauds and the class is clapping
and they're clapping and clapping for you
and they believe you are touched by God
and they believe that God has spoken through you
and they're hugging you and they're touching you
and they're saying "God loves you"
God has chosen you as a vessel
and this feels like the first time
you've ever been chosen
and for a moment everyone forgets
about that day you accidentally stabbed Jamie Kirk
in the arm with a number two pencil
because Eric Fisher memorized
the Ten Commandments before you did
and for today your performance made you the star
you were touched and loved and hugged
and you got a piece of paper that said
"Jeanette Powers has received a gold star
for the ability to speak in tongues."

"Amanda, because you can't say her name in English."
--Jeanette Powers

—I'm giving her all she's got, Captain!—
stubbornmulepress@gmail.com
jeanettepowers.com

www.ingramcontent.com/pod-product-compliance
Lightning Source LLC
Chambersburg PA
CBHW020034120526
44588CB00030B/422